This book belongs to :

....

This book
belongs to:

We become what we love and who we love shapes what we become.

St. Clare of Assisi

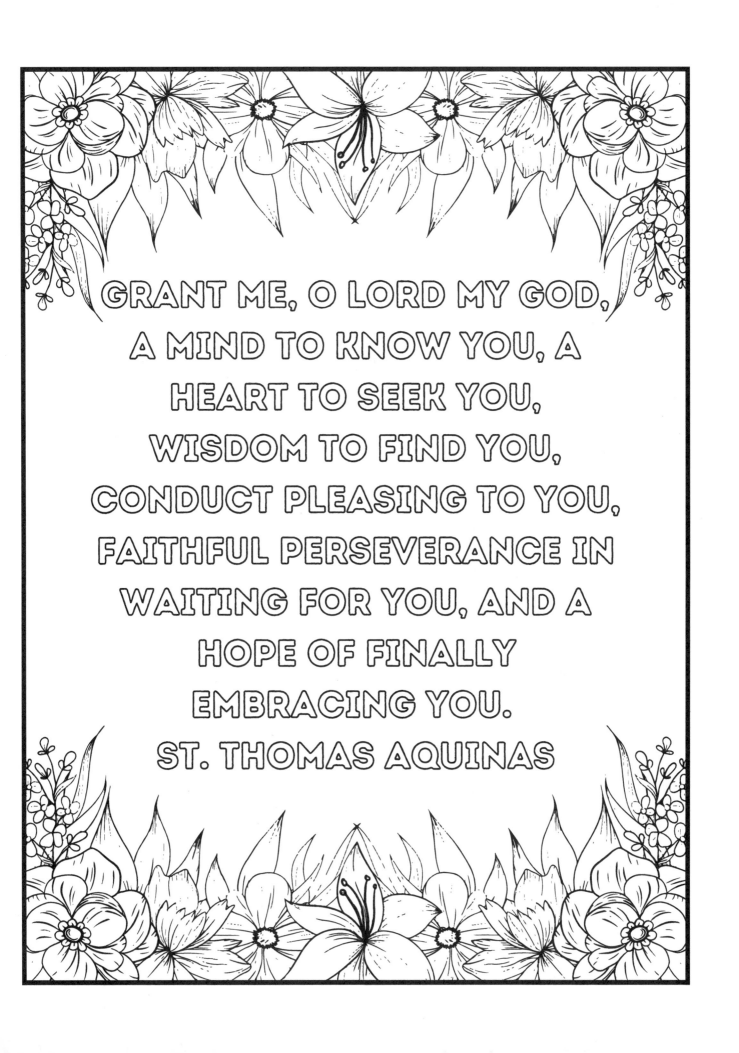

GRANT ME, O LORD MY GOD, A MIND TO KNOW YOU, A HEART TO SEEK YOU, WISDOM TO FIND YOU, CONDUCT PLEASING TO YOU, FAITHFUL PERSEVERANCE IN WAITING FOR YOU, AND A HOPE OF FINALLY EMBRACING YOU.
ST. THOMAS AQUINAS

Who except God can give you peace? Has the world ever been able to satisfy the heart?

St. Gerald Majella

Those who carry God in their hearts bear heaven with them wherever they go.
St. Ignatius of Loyola

Be who God meant you to be and you will set the world on fire.

St. Catherine of Siena

Christ has no body but yours,
No hands, no feet on earth but yours,
Yours are the eyes with which He looks
Compassion on this world,
Yours are the feet with which He walks to do good, Yours are the hands, with which He blesses all the world.
Yours are the hands, yours are the feet,
Yours are the eyes, you are His body.
Christ has no body now but yours,
No hands, no feet on earth but yours,
Yours are the eyes with which He looks compassion on this world.
Christ has no body now on earth but yours.

St. Teresa of Avila

Christ has no body but
yours,
No hands, no feet on
earth but yours,
Yours are the eyes with
which He looks
Compassion on this
world.
Yours are the feet with
which He walks to do
good, Yours are the
hands, with which He
blesses all the world.
Yours are the hands,
yours are the feet,
Yours are the eyes, you
are His Body.
Christ has no body now
but yours,
No hands, no feet on
earth but yours,
Yours are the eyes with
which He looks
compassion on this world.
Christ has no body now
on earth but yours.

St. Teresa of Avila.

We must always remember that God does everything well, although we may not see the reason of what He does.

St. Philip Neri

We must
always
remember that
God does
everything
well, although
we may not
see the reason
of what He
does.

St Philip Neri

We have been called to heal wounds, to unite what has fallen apart, and to bring home those who have lost their way.

St. Francis of Assisi

Nothing great is ever achieved without much enduring.

St. Catherine of Siena

Have caution in not allowing yourself to be struck down by adversity nor becoming vain by prosperity.
St. Clare of Assisi

The Creator of the universe awaits the prayer of one poor little person to save a multitude of others, redeemed like her at the price of His Blood.
St. Therese of Lisieux

The Creator of the universe
awaits the prayer of one
poor little person to save a
multitude of others!
redeemed like her at the
price of His Blood.

St. Therese of Lisieux

HELP ME TO JOURNEY BEYOND THE FAMILIAR AND INTO THE UNKNOWN. GIVE ME THE FAITH TO LEAVE OLD WAYS AND BREAK FRESH GROUND WITH YOU.
ST. BRENDAN OF CLONFERT

HELP ME TO JOURNEY BEYOND THE FAMILIAR AND INTO THE UNKNOWN. GIVE ME THE FAITH TO LEAVE OLD WAYS AND BREAK FRESH GROUND WITH YOU.

ST. BRENDAN OF CLONFERT

YOU HAVE MADE US FOR YOURSELF, O LORD, AND OUR HEARTS ARE RESTLESS UNTIL THEY REST IN YOU.
ST. AUGUSTINE OF HIPPO

I know well that the greater and more beautiful the work is, the more terrible will be the storms that rage against it.

St. Faustina Kowalska

It is Jesus that you seek when you dream of happiness; He is waiting for you when nothing else you find satisfies you.

St. John Paul II

Dismiss all anger and look into yourself a little. Remember that he of whom you are speaking is your brother, and as he is in the way of salvation, God can make him a saint, in spite of his present weakness. St. Thomas of Villanova

Pray with great confidence, with confidence based on the goodness and infinite generosity of God and upon the promises of Jesus Christ. God is a spring of living water which flows unceasingly into the hearts of those who pray.
St. Louis De Montfort

Pray with great confidence, with
confidence based on the goodness and
infinite generosity of God and upon the
promises of Jesus Christ. God is a spring
of living water which flows unceasingly
into the hearts of those who pray.

St. Louis De Montfort

Let nothing disturb you,
Let nothing frighten you,
All things are passing away:
God never changes.
Patience obtains all things
Whoever has God lacks
nothing;
God alone suffices.

St. Teresa of Avila

Let nothing disturb you.
Let nothing frighten you.
All things are passing away;
God never changes.
Patience obtains all things
Whoever has God lacks
nothing;
God alone suffices.
St. Teresa of Avila

No one,
however weak,
is denied a
share in the
victory of the
cross. No one is
beyond the help
of the prayer of
Christ.
St. Leo the Great

No one, however weak, is denied a share in the victory of the cross. No one is beyond the help of the prayer of Christ.

St. Leo the Great

It is a lesson we all need to let alone the things that do not concern us. He has other ways for others to follow Him; all do not go by the same path. It is for each of us to learn the path by which He requires us to follow Him, and to follow Him in that path.
St. Katharine Drexel

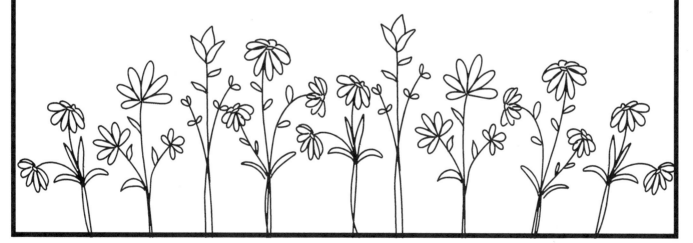

It is a lesson we all need to let
alone the things that do not
concern us. He has other ways for
others to follow Him; all do not go
by the same path. It is for each of
us to learn the path by which He
requires us to follow Him, and to
follow Him in that path.

St. Katharine Drexel

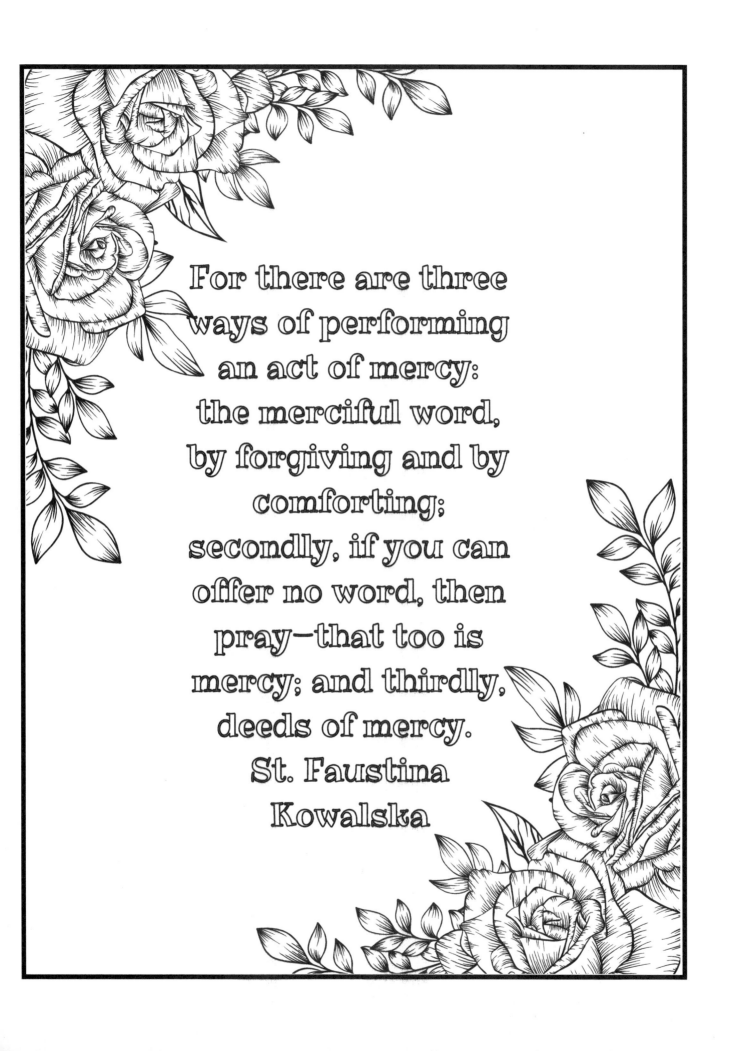

For there are three
ways of performing
an act of mercy:
the merciful word,
by forgiving and by
comforting;
secondly, if you can
offer no word, then
pray—that too is
mercy; and thirdly,
deeds of mercy.
St. Faustina
Kowalska

Lord, help me to make time today to serve you in those who are most in need of encouragement or assistance.
St. Vincent de Paul

Love takes up where knowledge leaves off. St. Thomas Aquinas

Love takes up where knowledge leaves off.

St. Thomas Aquinas

For prayer is nothing
else than being on
terms of friendship
with God.
St. Teresa of Avila

For prayer is nothing
else than being on
terms of friendship
with God.

St. Teresa of Avila

Our true worth does not consist in what human beings think of us. What we really are consists in what God knows us to be.
St. John Berchmans

Our true worth does not consist in what human beings think of us. What we really are consists in what God knows us to be.

St. John Berchmans

If you truly want to help the soul of your neighbor, you should approach God first with all your heart. Ask him simply to fill you with charity, the greatest of all virtues; with it you can accomplish what you desire.
St. Vincent Ferrer

We shall steer safely through every storm, so long as our heart is right, our intention fervent, our courage steadfast, and our trust fixed on God.

St. Francis de Sales

The life of the body is the soul; the life of the soul is God.

St. Anthony of Padua

The life of the body is the soul; the
life of the soul is God.

St. Anthony of Padua

I know God will not give me anything I can't handle. I just wish that he didn't trust me so much. St. Teresa of Calcutta

Help me to journey beyond the familiar and into the unknown. Give me the faith to leave old ways and break fresh ground with You.

St. Brendan of Clonfert

Help me to journey beyond the familiar and into the unknown. Give me the faith to leave old ways and break fresh ground with you.

St. Brendan of Clonfert

He will provide the way and the means, such as you could never have imagined. Leave it all to Him, let go of yourself, lose yourself on the Cross, and you will find yourself entirely.
St. Catherine of Siena

Holiness consists simply in doing God's will, and being just what God wants us to be.
St. Therese of Lisieux

Know that the greatest service that man can offer to God is to help convert souls.
St. Rose of Lima

We need no wings to go in search of God, but have only to find a place where we can be alone and look upon Him present within us.
St. Teresa of Avila

In tribulation immediately draw near to God with confidence, and you will receive strength, enlightenment, and instruction. St. John of the Cross

If we wish to make any progress in the service of God we must begin every day of our life with new eagerness. We must keep ourselves in the presence of God as much as possible and have no other view or end in all our actions but the divine honor.

St. Charles Borromeo

If we wish to make any progress in
the service of God we must begin
every day of our life with new
eagerness. We must keep
ourselves in the presence of God
as much as possible and have no
other view or end in all our actions
but the divine honor.
~ St. Charles Borromeo

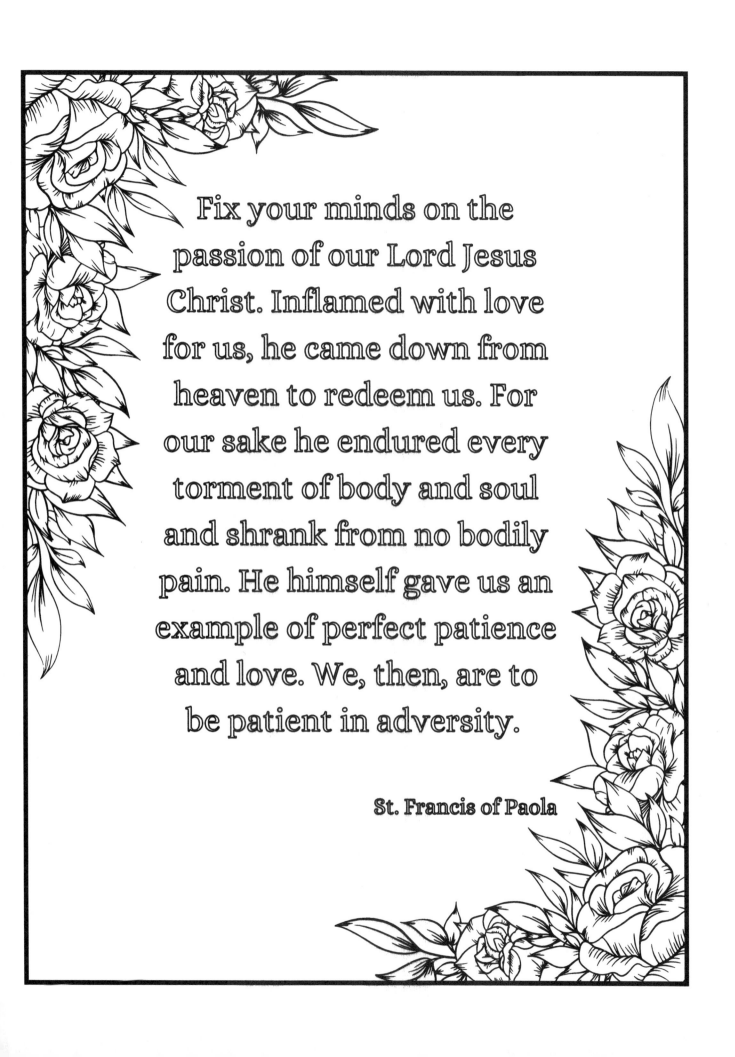

Fix your minds on the passion of our Lord Jesus Christ. Inflamed with love for us, he came down from heaven to redeem us. For our sake he endured every torment of body and soul and shrank from no bodily pain. He himself gave us an example of perfect patience and love. We, then, are to be patient in adversity.

St. Francis of Paola

By reason of His immensity, God is present everywhere; but there are two places where He dwells in a particular manner. One is in the highest heavens, where He is present by that glory which He communicates to the blessed; the other is on earth within the humble soul that loves Him.

St. Alphonsus Liguori

I will attempt day by day to break my will into pieces. I want to do God's Holy Will, not my own.
St. Gabriel Possenti

Nothing great is ever achieved without much enduring.

St. Catherine of Siena

Nothing great is ever achieved
without much enduring.

St. Catherine of Siena

Made in United States
Troutdale, OR
12/14/2024

26459733R00046